Born in 1861, Rabindranath Tagore was a key figure of the Bengal Renaissance. He started writing at an early age and by the turn of the century had become a household name in Bengal as a poet, a songwriter, a playwright, an essayist, a short story writer and a novelist. In 1913 he was awarded the Nobel Prize for Literature and his verse collection *Gitanjali* came to be known internationally. At about the same time he founded Visva-Bharati, a university located in Santiniketan, near Kolkata. Called the 'Great Sentinel' of modern India by Mahatma Gandhi, Tagore steered clear of active politics but is famous for returning his knighthood as a gesture of protest against the Jallianwala Bagh massacre in 1919.

Tagore was a pioneering literary figure, renowned for his ceaseless innovations in poetry, prose, drama, music and painting—which he took up late in life. His works include novels; plays; essays on religious, social and literary topics; some sixty collections of verse; over a hundred short stories; and more than 2,500 songs, including the national anthems of India and Bangladesh.

Rabindranath Tagore died in 1941. His eminence as India's greatest modern poet remains unchallenged to this day.

*

Samir Sengupta has written biographies of eminent Bengali writers and also translated and edited their works.

*

Debjani Banerjee holds a PhD and teaches in the areas of postcolonial literature and cultural studies. She has previously translated two books for Penguin. She lives in Bangalore and enjoys travelling.

THE NECTAR OF LIFE

Quotations from the Prose Writings

Rabindranath Tagore

Edited by Samir Sengupta
Translated by Debjani Banerjee

PENGUIN BOOKS

PENGUIN BOOKS

Published by the Penguin Group

Penguin Books India Pvt. Ltd, 11 Community Centre, Panchsheel Park,
New Delhi 110 017, India

Penguin Group (USA) Inc., 375 Hudson Street, New York, New York 10014, USA

Penguin Group (Canada), 90 Eglinton Avenue East, Suite 700, Toronto,
Ontario, M4P 2Y3, Canada (a division of Pearson Penguin Canada Inc.)

Penguin Books Ltd, 80 Strand, London WC2R 0RL, England

Penguin Ireland, 25 St Stephen's Green, Dublin 2, Ireland
(a division of Penguin Books Ltd)

Penguin Group (Australia), 250 Camberwell Road, Camberwell,
Victoria 3124, Australia (a division of Pearson Australia Group Pty Ltd)

Penguin Group (NZ), 67 Apollo Drive, Rosedale, Auckland 0632,
New Zealand (a division of Pearson New Zealand Ltd)

Penguin Group (South Africa) (Pty) Ltd, 24 Sturdee Avenue, Rosebank,
Johannesburg 2196, South Africa

Penguin Books Ltd, Registered Offices: 80 Strand, London WC2R 0RL, England

First published by Penguin Books India 2011

Copyright © Penguin Books India 2011

All rights reserved

10 9 8 7 6 5 4 3 2 1

ISBN 9780143415640

Typeset in Adobe Jenson Pro by SÜRYA, New Delhi
Printed at Anubha Printers, Noida

Contents

Editor's Note

Any compilation of quotations from Rabindranath Tagore is bound to be incomplete. Not only did this astonishing personality have an astounding variety of thoughts and opinions on just about every subject under the sun, but he had the exceptional ability to express his thoughts precisely and memorably in writing. Tagore had mastered so many means of communication that only his complete works can perhaps truly represent the extent of his thought. The reader is quite likely to complain that one or the other of his favourite quotations from Tagore is missing from this collection. Just before the book went to press, I was myself reminded of several memorable quotes and regretted not having included them.

However, one should clarify at the outset that this compilation does not have lofty ambitions. Some years ago, I had some compulsory leave; I read Rabindranath's prose anew and copied down some of his memorable lines. When I later showed these to some scholars, they suggested that I publish the collection—notable among them were Shankho Ghosh and Swapan Majumdar. The book was published with enthusiasm by Ananda Publishers in Bengali, and now it is made available to a wider audience by Penguin in English.

My hope is that in these pages readers will chance upon some wonderful quotations that they may not have come across before, or they may come upon a new interpretation of something they have read earlier. For readers who are new to Tagore, this small collection should provide an intriguing and enjoyable introduction. The quotations are divided into a series of thematic sections for the reader's convenience.

The sources for the quotations have been omitted from the English edition. Quotations from Tagore's novels, short stories and plays have not been used, since many of these lines are spoken by fictional characters and are often inextricably linked with the context of the fictional work. What have been used are extracts from Tagore's essays, travelogues, letters, some lectures and introductions.

ART

Curved lines represent life and human beings cannot control them easily. Straight lines are inert; human beings can discipline them easily and use them to carry heavy loads and take advantage of them.

To construct means to build to certain dimensions. What is being built is not the ultimate; it is important to build it to measurements and to one's own or other people's needs. Creating something, however, does not depend on dimensions. It is about realizing and expressing one's own self.

If we analyse a sculpture too much, we understand the material used but not the joy of the sculptor.

Many emotions float around in our mind. When these emotions become distinctive in rhythm and words, they become poetry and music. The joy is not because the emotions have been expressed; it is because the emotions have been made distinctive.

It is easy to prove that which can be proved but it is not easy to express something that is full of joy.

Our body bears the weight of our limbs but it is dependent on the limbs for its movement. When this paradox is resolved, dance is born.

When the infinite is within limits, it is a picture; when it is limitless, it is music.

Art expresses itself uniformly and skill through conflicts.

To be out of step with the whole is the basis of mockery.

There is no easy way to make others feel your own feelings. One can only use language to convey some information. If it is simply said that there was happiness, information is passed on, but the happiness is not shared.

The greatest power within human beings is the force of creativity.

In creative work, we should avoid the past and the present and rely on eternity.

The world of music and poetry has an eternal youth which is not always compatible with life.

Human beings have thirsts other than physical ones. Music, art and literature point to these other thirsts within the human heart.

Arguments about all kinds of art, between the educated and the uneducated, take different routes. One group asks, 'What would you understand?' The other group retorts angrily, 'How is it that you understand everything and no one else understands anything?'

The main function of art is to separate that which is pleasing to us from its own context within the world and present it with unmixed brilliance. It is the work of the artist to filter out that bit from the uppermost layer of truth and adorn it.

Art is not a loud shout; its true recognition is in its self-control. It can be silenced by pushing, but it will not embarrass itself by pushing forward in order to show off.

One of the main joys of art is freedom. It can take you very far, and after you come back to the mundane world, there is still a jingle in your ear and exhilaration within you.

The musicians of our country often do not remember that the main theory of art is in its economy; expressing beauty is its job. Finite boundaries make beauty truth; if those boundaries are crossed, art becomes distortion.

The artist cannot be tempted.

The aim of excellent art is not in moving people to tears or overwhelming them with emotion. Its aim is to transport the mind to that imaginary world where complete beauty can be realized.

Any composition within fine art begs the question: is it giving pleasure?

It is against the rules to spoil the harmony of art by indulging in excess.

One who creates expresses himself in many ways.

One who has truly studied art can look at unknown styles of art and recognize the aesthetics because he has developed an artistic perspective. Those who learn only by imitation cannot see beyond those imitations.

There are things like music to remind people that however clear and logical you want to make everything, there are some inner truths that cannot be articulated, but which are linked to the expression of our souls. These are the truths that cause us so much joy and sorrow and so much agitation.

More than other forms of art, acting relies on mimicking, but even so it is not mere ventriloquism. It has taken the responsibility to remove the veil from what appears to be normal and probe within. If we try too hard to keep things normal, we tend to cover up what is within.

The joy of looking at a painting is the joy of witnessing the familiar. We see the infinite through the etching of controlled lines. The mind cries out: I have definitely seen. I may have seen a pebble, a donkey, cactus, an old woman or any other thing. Where I can see clearly, I touch infinity and am overjoyed.

When we want to give information through language, our sole responsibility is to retain the truth of the narrative. When we want to create something, the rhythm is more important than the truth.

The rules of rhyme are created by God; they are not the fetters of the blacksmith.

The essence of rhythm is in the pause because the pause does not deter rhythm; it makes it more regular.

Dance is respected as a way of expressing emotion and thus is a part of art education in all countries. In our country, this has not been a custom in genteel society and therefore we assume that we have no tradition in dance.

The objective of speed is to be focused and move forward. Dance wants to express itself through movement in a variety of ways.

There is something more important than craftsmanship: emotion.

The devotee of Saraswati creates a picture. The devotee of Lakshmi acquires it, not because he has the right, but because he has money in the bank.

One cannot say that the Japanese cannot use swords, but they take up the brush with equal ease and skill.

We human beings can see our radiant inner selves within our creations. That is why we love the art of artists and the poetry of poets.

The mechanic prays to his machine, the warrior to his sword and the musician to his veena. It is not that they do not know the instruments as objects. However, they also know that the machine is only part of the instrument; the joy and sense of accomplishment they get out of the instruments are not the work of the wood or the iron alone.

BEAUTY

What do we call beautiful? It is that which on the outside may be commonplace, but when its inner meaning is understood, its beauty is revealed.

That which is beautiful carries the passport of God; it has unrestricted entry everywhere.

Why do we compare beauty to dreams? Perhaps we want to describe beauty without the weight of reality.

Beauty is beyond the extreme reach of the senses; not only the eyes and the ears, beauty can overwhelm even the heart.

Logic has its own dictionary and even its own grammar but our taste or aesthetics does not yet have its own grammar.

The beauty of the road is not in the grass or the flowers but in its vast, uninterrupted expanse. It is enjoyable not because of the buzzing of the bees, but because of the untiring footsteps of the travellers.

Beautiful things are not beautiful because they benefit us; they benefit us because they are beautiful.

All that is great and sublime in the world is surrounded by emptiness. Its background is simple. It does not want to take the help of anything else to showcase itself.

The thing that is truly beautiful must have a lot of empty space around it. Crowding together beautiful objects is like asking the virtuous wife to live with her husband along with other co-wives.

People want to beautify objects of daily use like utensils because their beauty signifies the taste and joy of their lives. The use of utensils indicates human needs while their beauty indicates the aesthetic sense of human beings.

There are few things as beautiful amongst human creations as a sailboat. Where human beings have consented to move along with the rhythm of nature, the beauty of their creations is inevitable.

The beauty of illusion is to be dressed in spring flowers but the beauty of freedom is unadorned.

It has not been proved so far that beauty is absolutely necessary for our lives, or that those civilizations who are more artistic are more powerful and have more life force in them.

Those who cannot truly immerse themselves in beauty dismiss beauty as something merely sensual.

You will be blind to real beauty if you disrespect it.

Beauty is that which contains a unity of ideas which is beyond analysis.

The waves of the sea are beautiful and the sounds of the sea are pleasing to the ear. But if one does not know how to swim, it would be wise to sit on the shore and enjoy both.

CIVILIZATION

All races have their excesses and exaggerations but those of others seem incongruous and ours seem perfectly justified.

All societies have had to fight against nature; civilization is the wealth that has been obtained through that fight.

Through conflicts, human beings move from elementary to more composite forms of living and this is called civilization.

The heart of civilization is that human beings interact with one another for their common good.

We now know that the telegraph, railways and impressive schools are not the true ingredients or symbols of civilization, and therefore we must look elsewhere to understand the goals of humanity. Then we may come to realize that to understand humanity we are not required to follow western military ideals.

Nowadays it seems that civilization has no responsibility to prove itself as civilized.

Europe considers Asia as not only different but also inferior.

Those who feel proud to have imitated the Europeans are actually imitating European manners. It is easy to copy this as it is the exterior of a person but to copy the person within is difficult.

Just as the Brahmin has the sacred thread, the England-returned individual has his clothes, and these set him apart in the same way as a caste mark does.

Nowadays, the circumstances are such that one wonders if European civilization will last beyond tomorrow. What they call patriotism will destroy them.

We calculate dates and say that there is no civilization as old as ours. But dates are a mathematical calculation and not an account of life force. By the same token, ashes can also make some arithmetical calculations and come to the conclusion that they are the oldest fire.

If we look into reasons for the destruction of civilization, we can find only one: distortion and interruption of human relationships.

Cities are dense with activity; any space here becomes emptiness. As soon as there is free time, we want to cover it up with alcohol and cards—otherwise the time does not seem to pass. In other words, we do not want time; we want to spend it.

CULTURE

The problem is that if one does not have taste, one cannot be made to understand what it is.

If sandesh is swallowed whole like a quinine pill, the thing is eaten but not tasted.

It is not necessary to explain the meaning of taste to the person who has taste; those who do not have that power need not delve into any of this.

Those who are delighted by taste, grace and beauty are outnumbered by those who are impressed by bravado.

I have not had the experience of meeting a person without taste who is fully aware that he has no taste.

A sense of humour can be a dangerous thing; if it comes easily and with grace, it is a good thing. But if it is forced, then it can become a distortion.

Humour has two main ingredients: promptness and distinctiveness.

Arguments about liking and not liking a particular thing are more tiring than other conflicts.

Vulgarity can affect the mind easily and forcefully. Those who are weak and do not have time can be easily and cheaply entertained through vulgarity.

The flame of European culture can spark civilization in the outer world but it cannot show the way.

We understand a man not from what he knows but from what he enjoys.

If you cannot enjoy the best things in life, it is something to be ashamed of, not to take pride in.

EDUCATION

The most important aspect of education is not explanation; it is to ignite the mind.

The mind is more important than what is external; this should be a child's first lesson.

The sign of a good education is that it does not astound people but it gives them freedom.

In all great countries, the immediate goal of education is to get practical opportunities; its higher objective is the ultimate fulfilment of human lives. Universities have evolved naturally from these objectives.

In no country is education fully obtained from schools. It is the same in our country. The ability to cook is not made in the sweetmeat shop; only the sweet is made there.

Lack of education is the basis of all the ills in India today. Caste discrimination, religious conflict, lack of enterprise, economic instability—all of these stem from ignorance.

That students develop distaste for education is not primarily because the subject is difficult but because the method of instruction is dull.

There is nothing as dangerous to a child as listless teaching. It gives little and takes much away from the mind.

Everyone seems to think that if education is full of hardship, it will be fruitful. However, the way the heart of a child will blossom through joy and the breeze of logic is incomparable.

Our biggest need today is equality in education.

If exams are passed by learning by rote, is it not cheating? If we take the book concealed within our clothes it is cheating. But isn't it also cheating if we take the matter in our brain without understanding it?

Children need nature in their growing years while they are learning. Trees, clear blue skies, the breeze, clean water and panoramic views are as important as school benches, books and examinations.

There is a lesson in trying to read human beings instead of books. Through this, one learns something; more importantly, the power of learning is developed in a way that school lessons cannot enable.

If we do not let people make mistakes, we do not let them learn something.

Whichever route we follow, we will arrive at the conclusion that teaching is imparted by a teacher and not by a method.

If you cannot respect students, it will be difficult for students to respect you.

Those who should have been jailors, drill sergeants or exorcists should not take up the responsibility of helping students develop. They who are young at heart, enjoy learning and can respect the weak should be doing this job.

Getting an education does not depend solely on the educational institution. It depends primarily on the student. Many students go to the university and get degrees but they do not get an education.

There is no point in teaching a mind that is already mature. When the mind is young and ready to absorb nutrients, it can assimilate knowledge and ideas and make itself vital, strong and able.

The easiest way to escape an examination is to pass it.

FAME

We are all moving from nothingness towards fulfilment and of course we have not reached our final goal yet. But whenever in life we have built something that lasts, we have done so through our moral principles and not through depravity.

When we see a poet who has earned fame during his lifetime, we begin to doubt the veracity of his fame.

Since fame is usually attained after death, does it matter if that fame is true or false?

One has to admit that fame has its own intoxication; but like all other forms of intoxication, this one too can bring weariness and fatigue.

Nobody is forced to respect themselves; however, one must respect an eminent man.

It is easy to accept an honour but difficult to maintain it.

FREEDOM

If we cannot be independent by our zeal and force, no one can give us our freedom. What is offered as freedom is only bondage in another guise.

We often mistake new bondages for freedom.

There is no independence outside of the independence of the soul.

Just as freedom is to be aspired towards, subjugation also needs to be striven for. Perhaps the ultimate and most superior form of bondage is called freedom.

When freedom first proclaims itself, it breaks rules. Afterwards, it creates its own rules and only then can it be truly brought under control.

Every person is born with the message of freedom, the freedom to move from darkness into light.

Those who try to use shackles to bind tend to lose! Those who give freedom are able to keep.

If a boat does not have a rudder, it cannot boast of being independent because it is at the mercy of countless waves.

We want independence but we do not believe in freedom.

Human beings often say this one surprising thing: I want freedom. What do they want freedom from?

Where human beings are completely alone, they are completely independent.

Freedom is not an external thing, but a thing of the mind. Therefore, we cannot get it from someone else. Until we get that independence through our inner, natural strength, external powers will bind us, harness and dominate us.

GOD

We can pride ourselves on the few pennies in our pocket but we cannot boast of what God has given us. We can enjoy the firmament full of golden light for which we can never repay Him, but we cannot boast about it.

There is one thing that I can give God. If we give Him flowers or water, these things belong to Him. Only if I can give Him my will, it would be giving Him something that belongs to me.

The will of God may not be rushed but it certainly is infallible.

When music plays, we forget all our problems and we can see the Musician of the instrument of our life. At such times, sorrow does not overwhelm us and loss does not impoverish us. In the joy of the Musician, we glimpse the ultimate meaning of our lives. That vision gives us salvation.

God's wealth is His will; will is the prologue to creation.

God is not far away; he is not in the church but within us. He exists silently amidst births and deaths, joys and sorrows, good and evil. The world is His permanent temple.

We feel the first stirrings of the pain of anxiety when God, quietly, touches the edge of our consciousness.

If we think that we attain virtue through praying to God, then too we are not sacrificing everything at His feet; a substantial part is hoarded for our own virtue.

GREATNESS

We cannot achieve anything great by begging.

Sometimes deprivation is so deep that there is no awareness of deprivation, and barriers are so insurmountable that people begin to see the barriers as shelters. It is at such extraordinary times that a messiah appears!

Greatness can often be accompanied by lack of beauty which does not seem repugnant; in fact, it can attract the mind.

The predominant difference between great and ordinary people is that great people can live, for the most part, in their inner world where there is independence; for ordinary people, that space is difficult to enter or even unknown.

It does not take much imagination to think of oneself as great. But to understand the greatness of a truly great person takes heightened imaginative powers.

We must leave a lot of space for that which is valuable and great. Emptiness is most important to experience greatness fully.

Greatness comes out of the conflict of opposites. The tenets of Christianity are opposed to European character; the essence of European character has been churned through this religion and thus strengthened.

When smallness gets an exalted rank, it threatens, boasts and blusters. What this means is that it has not learnt the lesson of greatness.

Greatness has to face criticism every step of the way. One who is discouraged by such censure will not get the epithet of 'hero'.

When we show respect to the undeserving, we demean the truly great man; the difference between gods and demi-gods is erased.

The natural affinity of the soul is towards greatness. Regardless of what they say, people trust greatness.

True humility comes when a person forgets the reasons for his greatness. If he is conscious of not appearing boastful, that is not true humility.

Just because a mosquito can trouble an elephant does not mean the mosquito is greater than the elephant.

The peak of the Himalayas and its base are at different levels. A truly great man can be measured by the hostility of the circumstances he faces.

HAPPINESS

There is no one thing called happiness. No one can collect happiness like a precious jewel, put it in a bottle, place it securely on one's person and claim, 'That's done! There is nothing more.' Happiness is in the cultivation of strange and interesting human propensities; it is to be found in the flow of life.

If we must truly enjoy something, we need to surround it with leisure on all sides.

One cannot bypass unpleasantness; the best method is to push it away by force. If you walk along the side of a river, you will never cross it. One must jump into the river, swim against the tide with all one's might and only then can the dry land on the other side be reached.

The novel comes with the surprise of suddenness but things that are truly new bring with them everlasting happiness.

True joy comes from expressing oneself fully. A talented man may find his work difficult but he will also find joy in it. A mother may have to work with troublesome children but a true mother will find joy in it.

When we get something without having given anything, it is like begging. There is no happiness and no respect in this.

Happiness is an everyday thing but joy exceeds the daily and the mundane. Happiness cringes from grime but joy celebrates in dust and destroys its differences with the universe.

Dust is unimportant to happiness but it adorns joy.

Happiness is afraid of loss but joy finds satisfaction in sharing everything; this is why having nothing is poverty for happiness but for joy poverty is wealth.

The difference between happiness and joy is that the opposite of happiness is sorrow but the opposite of joy is not sorrow. Just as Shiva swallowed the poison, joy takes in sorrow with the same ease. In fact, it is through sorrow that joy fulfills itself and realizes its completeness.

Happiness is not for the feeble-minded; it is earned by hard work and strength.

People have to get together in a celebration. We cannot celebrate alone.

Illness and unhappiness can make us failures but happiness and prosperity make people petty.

HINDUISM

A unique mixture has arisen from the mingling of the purist theoretical knowledge of the Aryans and the taste and creative impulse of the Dravidians. Not completely Aryan or non-Aryan, this is Hindu culture.

Although we, numerous Aryans and non-Aryans and other mixed groups, have forged an unprecedented unity, we have not been strengthened by it. We are as divided as we are unified.

Traditions are the way human beings make connections among themselves; it is here that Hindus have erected fences at every step along the way.

Hindus are, and at the same time are not, considered a specific nation. They have the narrowness of nationalism but not its strength.

If discriminating between people is wrong, then it is wrong for the entire Hindu society. It is, therefore, an anti-Hindu practice.

Hindu society is vast but weak; its ties are at once firm and flexible, and its boundaries are as undefined as they are rigid.

In Hindu society, it is wrong to kill a cow; however, if for the sake of a cow, human beings are killed, it is not so wrong. We punish people if they have food with Muslims, but we will not punish them if they cause harm to the same people.

The advent of the Brahmo religion is a part of the history of Hindu religion. It is born of the conflicts within the Hindu religion, through tremendous strength that seeks to fulfil a dire need. The advent of the Brahmo Samaj is neither sudden nor abrupt.

If, in order to fulfil a task, we try to forget that Hindus and Muslims are separate, reality will never let us forget it.

Muslims have a specific religion but Hinduism is not that structured a religion. It is the racial culmination of the history of India.

I agree that if Bankimchandra's song *Vande mataram* is read in its entirety, in line with his other historical novels, it can be interpreted in ways that can hurt the sentiments of Muslims.

HISTORY

The history of human beings is composed by particular individuals.

The self and other, earning and giving up, freedom and control, rituals and judgement—human beings are constantly pulled along contrary directions. To learn the lesson of humanity is to learn how to balance both these pulls. To learn the history of balancing is to know the history of humankind.

Our history is a choir of the lives of great people.

In our country, the main difference that can be made between the educated and the uneducated is in the knowledge of history.

It is unfortunate that the history that we study makes us Indians seem unimportant; it is the invaders who are everything.

According to modern, western definitions, the Mahabharata may not be history—but it is indeed a true history of the Aryans.

We do not have to accept the stories in the Mahabharata as factual but I think they are based on true ideas. If we look for facts here we may be deceived, but we shall certainly find truth.

History has shown over and over again that great things do not come into being on their own.

The English gave us some fire of knowledge but there is too much smoke accompanying it. That increases our darkness and blinds us further.

The entry of the British into Indian history is a curious event. As human beings, they stayed further away from us than even the Muslims; yet as the moral messengers of Europe they have entered our psyche extensively and in depth in a way that no other foreign power has been able to.

HUMANITY

If humanity is alive within us, we can understand concepts of humanity that are ancient and modern, eastern or western.

We harbour many enemies and many vices within our bodies. If we analyse all of them, we will find that each person has many disorders. However, the overall health that shines through by defeating these disorders is what is crucial.

Human beings cannot let go of the belief that where there is a wish for well-being, there will also be power to bring in good.

That which insults human dignity cannot be the way to progress.

If we cannot accept that there is an ideal that does more than fill our stomachs or make profits, then we belittle ourselves.

To be able to forgive human beings, one must first understand them.

An ideal that is truly great is not linked to a space or time. It bestows humanity on human beings. Human beings imbued with these ideals can sustain their excellence under any circumstances.

All human beings experience the dual pull of youthful spirit and mature fears. Fear says, 'Wait, watch,' and spirit says, 'Let's take the leap.'

If someone does welfare work, he will work for his own welfare. This is the ideal.

It is very difficult for the person who has nothing to accept charity.

We find a great deal of ourselves within others.

We have to stay together but we cannot be one—there is nothing more damaging than this.

People in a city cannot bond in an intimate relationship. We do not have to go far for an example. In Kolkata, neighbours do not have any relations in sadness or in trouble. We do not even know the names of our neighbours.

I was born in Kolkata and yet I cannot find a safe haven there. I have a house there but I cannot see anything as my own. If human beings cannot find refuge, what is the point of having monuments and big edifices? Who is calling us there? It is the right place for businessmen.

Machines can do work but they cannot make human beings.

Sometimes mistakes can breed truth but machines can never produce human beings.

We cannot protect humanity when we cannot fill the stomachs of our people.

The stranglehold of a large family does not allow us to group as a race, as a country, or even develop our excellence as human beings. There are parents, sons, brothers, wives; in reaction to these social forces, there are those who have renounced domesticity. However, no one is born for the larger world; we refer to the family as the world.

Those who are true travellers belong to a different race as it were. Their bodies and minds are always in motion and they can negotiate easily in unfamiliar spaces.

The ability to come close to a human being is a rare ability.

We cannot make anything permanent out of pity.

If we try to help someone from the outside, the effort can get distorted at every step. Only when we are equal to the people we want to help is it possible to help them truly.

We are all human beings. If relations between us are not humane, simple and gentle, it is odd.

When a person I know barely is sitting next to me, there is a huge gap between us. The gap is of unconsciousness, of reluctance. If that person becomes an intimate friend, then I close the gap.

The child is the most ancient creation. Adults have undergone many changes depending on their country, time and education. But children are still the same as they were thousands of years ago.

The unfortunate child who gets too many toys cannot enjoy his playtime.

Showing affection is more for the parents; children find it troublesome.

A child will play with anything, anywhere. Through that we see play in its purest form. The cost of the toy and the excitement generated are superfluous and not connected to the child's play.

Human beings can easily forgive a familiar wrong even if it is a grave one. However, if the mistake is an unfamiliar one, it is hard to tolerate.

It is important for human beings to disbelieve. This may be a positive attribute as well. If we are to protect humanity, we must keep alive this ability to doubt.

Like courage, shame can also give strength. It is not impossible for a person to sacrifice his life out of shame.

Man is a spiritual being; he has a body, a mind and a heart. If he is to be satisfied, he has to be satisfied in each of these ways.

We can recognize human beings through their extravagance. People spend money in fixed ways but they overspend on their whims.

A wild elephant is like the embodiment of destruction. Ordinary man, whose size is barely comparable to the foot of the elephant, sees it and says, 'I will roam about on his back.' It is strange that at some point in time, a diminutive man had seen this gigantic creature advance with a raised trunk and had yet been able to imagine this.

Impractical, emotional people can be easily recognized by other people. However, they cannot see through other people in the same way.

In human nature, fear is worse than emptiness, ignorance and foolishness.

Those who are not known for brave deeds highlight their inabilities with blustering words.

The rule of the mediocre is the most intolerable for human beings.

The modesty of the great is natural and the weak must be humble. But it is the mediocre who are the most unbearable.

Generosity often depends upon a full stomach.

The fire of worry is as comfortable as the fire on a cold wintry day; it stays next to you but does not scorch.

Human beings tend to roll down the slope of convenience.

What human beings have got easily makes them equal to other creatures; what a person has earned through arduous practice makes him human.

Man, like God, has infinite desire but unlike God, he does not have infinite power.

Even the most timid person will laugh off the fear of ghosts in broad daylight; however, on a dark night, the rustle of a dry leaf, the shadow of a blade of grass can take control of our hearts. That false fear can dominate us more than real fear.

It is better to have faith and be cheated than misjudge someone by doubting him.

Many people are in the habit of fishing in a pond that contains no fish; eventually, it is not catching the fish but the hope that becomes an addiction.

We do not have the brute strength to keep our disbelief fully alive. We want to forget and be free of worries; somehow, we want to believe.

IDEAS

We all have the right to express our opinion but we do not have the right to force it on others.

It is our illusion to think that ideas are any less than reality.

We can easily pluck wise words from someone else's mouth like over-ripe fruit; however, it is very difficult to create the smallest thing with one's own words.

The part of the cup that is made of clay is not the important part; the part that is empty is the essence. The empty part can be filled with juices; the burnt clay is only incidental.

When an idea becomes separated from our feelings and is connected only to our knowledge, it loses dynamism. Then it is difficult to save the idea from certain death.

There is novelty in everyday thoughts and imagination which is obstructed by other, external novelties.

We have limited life and our joys and sorrows are transient. However, the flow of ideas that began in ancient times has coursed through thousands of minds and is still flowing along towards infinity.

We have different opinions and we will continue to have them; this is best.

Thought may be important but it will be defeated by tangible objects.

In Europe, ideas are the essence of people's lives. Even in dire need they look for ideas and therefore ideas come to them from the deepest recesses of their being.

It is very easy to mock great ideas.

IMAGINATION

The imagination necessary to enter into one's innermost feelings is the poetic imagination. Then there is a shortcut to being imaginative—to try and become scholarly without reading or to become a poet without feeling. This imagination has only surface glitter and is fraudulent.

Every human being has a sense of deep estrangement within himself. The One we want to be united with resides on the remote shores of His heavenly lake. We cannot travel there with our tangible bodies, but we can send our imagination to that point.

Being imaginative and being fanciful are two different things. Imagination is structured by reason, control and truth; fancy pretends to be truthful but is puffed up by strange excesses.

The joy of children is the purest form of joy. They can take a trivial incident and turn it into something important using their imagination. They can breathe life into an ugly, ragged doll with their own joys and sorrows. One who can retain this power as an adult is said to be imaginative.

It is difficult to compose dreams.

There is no harm in imagining strength as a lion; however, if we imagine only the lion as the symbol of strength then the power of imagination is undermined.

Mystery shelters unknown fears.

INDIA

The realization of one within many and the creation of unity amidst diversity—this is the essential spirit of India.

At a time when the massive Kurukshetra war was imminent, only a country like India could listen to the entire Bhagavad Gita and understand it. There is no other country like it in the world.

In other countries, religious beliefs are subject to the scriptures, but food, travel and daily rituals are independent. In India, there is much freedom in religious belief, but for food, travel and daily rituals, we adhere to the scriptures.

In Egypt, Turkey, Iraq and Persia, religion is giving way to humanity. Only in India, there is a thick growth of thorn bushes in the boundaries between Muslims and Hindus.

When we read the Mahabharata, we realize that in those times our civilization was full of vitality and strength. There was so much change, revolution and conflict of oppositional forces. It was certainly not a manicured, homogenous and mechanical society that was built by someone clever.

For hundreds of years, we have infected human beings with the poison of humiliation. We have burdened so many people with inferiority; today, the country is weighed down and enervated by this shame.

When small feet were thought to be beautiful, Chinese women bound and cut their feet by artificial means; but they got distorted, not beautiful, feet. Similarly, if India now tries to imitate European ideals suddenly, and by force, then we will get a distorted India.

We can imagine that Mother India is sitting on a rugged peak of the Himalayas and playing heart-rending tunes on her veena, but that is a dream. There is another Mother India who is sitting in a malaria-ridden village, next to a muddy pond, staring at her empty medicine stores while a dying son lies on her lap. If we glimpse this Mother India, we have seen reality.

The national anthem of India should not only be for the Hindus but also for the Muslims, Christians and Brahmos. Everyone should be able to join in with respect.

India, once non-vegetarian, has become vegetarian in most parts. This is a rare example in history.

No one has described our country adequately; as a result, we live here but know very little about it.

Our relatives are those we know well. When we, Indians, know one another intimately, we will be a great race.

I am a Bengali, not a Bedouin. I will skulk in a corner, judge and argue, change my mind several times, over and over, like fried fish sizzles in hot oil.

The biggest problem in our country is that we cannot consolidate anything; teamwork does not follow resolve. If, perchance, we can build a team in the morning, it will surely split by evening. This is our only enemy.

We Indians stay engrossed in an endeavour, like a child is absorbed in play, as long as there is no sacrifice involved. When the time comes to give up something, we make excuses and quit.

Our big ventures burst like big bubbles. At the start, there is much enthusiasm, but after a day or two, it loses momentum, gets distorted and with time becomes listless.

Only in our country is it possible to ask why one must go out. We seem to have forgotten that all human beings have a natural wish to step out of the house.

Hundreds of people within the country eat food that is inedible including barley–rice; they drink alcohol made from barley. This does not worry too many people. The greater concern seems to be about maintaining the strictures about eating pure food when they go abroad.

We have distanced ordinary people from our lives and yet, when we need them, we complain that they do not come forward to join us.

We have never given any evidence that we are the true well-wishers of Muslims or of ordinary people. Hence, when they are sceptical of our benevolence we cannot blame them.

Our countrymen do not get anything from one another. Water, food, education—we are dependent on the government for all of these. This is where our country is losing its way.

Ever since English education has been prevalent in our country, there has been a wide divide, akin to caste distinction, between those who know English and those who do not.

Naturally, the administrative laws of another homogenous nation cannot be applicable to India. The laws will evolve here through many conflicts.

The difference between one state and another is not only in location and language but also deeply ingrained in the mind. The interpersonal relationships between them are loose and often oppositional.

Unlike Europe, our masses do not live in cities. Like China, our people mainly dwell in the villages. The English, with their urban outlook, have cut our intimate ties with the rural areas. Therefore, our decline has started from the roots. There is so much poverty, misery, blindness and such helplessness in the villages.

INTELLIGENCE

W e can define what we can restrict within a boundary. But that which is infinite can only be understood by our perception and not by our intelligence.

Instinct takes the right path but intelligence travels helter-skelter, making many mistakes. Animals go by instinct and human beings by intelligence. Instinct travels within a small perimeter, the final goal of intelligence has not been discovered yet.

Genius is that energy force which has its roots in its own joy, not in external rules, motivation or temptations.

If it is important to stimulate our intelligence and creativity before a creation, then it is also important to keep completely silent for a long time.

It is not always true that varying levels of intelligence cause differences of opinion. In most cases, this may be caused by differences in nature.

Extraordinary intelligence has one problem; it is not able to explain as well as it understands.

The glory of human beings is that they are not solely dependent on their physical powers. They also rely on their intelligence, which has creative powers.

KNOWLEDGE

To understand everything clearly from start to finish is not the greatest gain.

Knowledge that is idle and unenterprising is not very useful. When knowledge moves with a specific purpose, it becomes wisdom.

Studying astronomy takes us to the centre of the mysterious universe where we are less weighed down by the problems of life.

The person who knows a lot can explain himself in a few words; the person who knows little needs to say a lot that is superfluous.

Learning that is premised upon somehow putting things together in a shallow manner is for the lazy person; it goes hand in glove with lack of learning.

We understand a lot of things but it takes considerable reflection to understand what it is that we have understood.

The biggest ignorance is ignorance about one's own lack of knowledge.

Our teachers are often intent on proving their old age; it is often an easy way to show one's authority.

Giving ethical counsel is like a dispute. It cannot be pleasant under any circumstances. Those who are being advised are being placed in the criminal's box. The advice either flies over their head or crashes against it.

Knowledge is the biggest unifier of people. An educated person in Bengal will have more similarity with an educated person in some corner of Europe than with his illiterate neighbour.

Those who sit on the school benches in English-medium schools and learn by rote are blinded to learning as a bright gleam of light; to them, the country is only the educated class, the peacock is its tail and the elephant is its tusks.

Many of us earn a lot of degrees but we do not gain enough knowledge.

Not only does knowledge help us learn many things, it also helps us know ourselves better.

LANGUAGE

Language is like the flowing stream of a river; we cannot inscribe the name of a person on it.

Language is not an inanimate object like gold or silver which can be set into a mould. It is lively; it can take on and reject in the name of a life force.

When language does not flow clearly, when it has to be carried with great effort, we cannot create lyrics and narratives with it.

If the grammar of a language is complete, that language is as good as dead.

Newly coined words, like new shoes, are uncomfortable in the beginning.

Using an interpreter is an arduous task; it is like digging every step of the way as we move forward.

We acquire important information through the English language but Sanskrit has something that gives us joy. It colours the horizon of our minds; it has a deep message. Like nature, it gives us peace and affords dignity to our thoughts.

We are born in the laps of our mothers and mother tongues. Both mothers are, for us, life-giving and absolutely necessary.

The Bengali language is full of gestures. I do not know any other language that has such a literary mode of expression.

It is wrong to call your great-grandmother your mother. Similarly, if we assume that only Sanskritized Bengali is Bengali, then that can show scholarship but it also reveals lack of common sense.

We can accept the word 'criminal' into the Bengali language instead of trying to translate it.

I cannot accept the word 'compulsory'. Using that terrible word is like insulting the codes of civilized language.

I really dislike the exclamation mark. The surprise and excitement communicated by the exclamation mark is an emotion. If this has not been conveyed in the writer's language, we cannot rent a punctuation mark to cover that lack.

The immature writer cannot rest until he does strange antics with language including the use of excessive gestures. The natural abilities of the creator are exceeded and the writing is marred by transgressions of truth and beauty.

Nothing is as funny to our countrymen as when we make a mistake while speaking English. Through this, the shame of our subjugation reflects more darkly.

When the Englishman at the end of a letter writes 'yours truly' it is made clear to me that truly he is not mine.

For us, English is a language of work, not emotion.

LIFE

Whatever the circumstance, one should neither trivialize the goal of life nor demean oneself in any way. Materialistic people are caught up in narrow webs that should not be respected.

The most important things that we get in this life are those that come without a price; we need not even bargain for them.

It is not easy to know ourselves. The main thread running through the various experiences of our life cannot be understood in a straightforward manner.

We can know life by experiencing it but we cannot contain it through definitions.

The true endeavour in life is to strive towards immortality; that is, to live on through something beyond death.

If we do not show signs of life, we do not have the right to bring in new lives. If we were lifeless, plants, animals, birds and insects would devour us. In this world, the lifeless cannot survive. They vanish within those who have life force.

Tension can reduce life span like nothing else.

When life is confined within narrow limits, instinct can be important. But in wider spheres, we need complete education of the mind, body and soul.

The life of human beings is like the journey of a river; one end of it is in the mountain peak/birth and the other in the sea/death. The two extremes are dark mysteries and in between we have work and achievements, which are like the noisy flow of the river. This cycle is unending.

Humanity is all about excess. Excess is the main objective of human life.

LITERATURE

Literature does not belong to an individual; it does not belong to the creator. It is like the voice of God.

The objective of literature is literature.

If a lotus is asked, 'Why do you exist?' it will reply, 'I exist for the sake of existence.' True literature, too, has the same reply.

Literature is a natural expression of life; it is not made out of necessity.

The external world and human characters take on certain forms in the mind of an individual. These forms create a pattern and music, which when expressed in words is called literature.

Literature has no overt consequences but it makes human nature more aware. It widens the scope of the human mind; where, earlier, the mind had no control, it begins to gain command.

The heart is eager to express itself. Thus, human beings have always had the urge to create literature.

Only literature can connect one human being to another, past to present and that which is distant to that which is near.

In literature we want the truth of life but not its responsibilities.

One function of all literature is to give importance to the audience. The audience helps shape the literature. Otherwise, the power of the writer is diminished.

People can learn from literature if they want. However, literature does not try to educate people; in no country has literature taken on the role of a schoolteacher.

Whatever gives joy is beautiful and that is the stuff of literature.

Pictures and music are the main ingredients of literature. Pictures give shape to ideas and music gives a rhythm. Pictures are like the body while music is the soul of literature.

All human beings are eager to have creative powers. When they find someone who helps them express their creativity, they repay their debt by making him famous.

The writer achieves immortality when he experiences the joy of success within himself.

The creation belongs to the writer alone. It will be different for each writer. Therefore, the writer stays alive through his creations and not through his emotions or his subject matter.

There are many tasks that can be accomplished through teamwork but literature is not one of them. Literature is the creation of one man alone.

The talent of a good writer is natural but that power should be honed by regular practice. When natural talent is combined with practice, it gives birth to truly good writing.

We do not hold authors accountable and therefore authors continue to be lethargic and try to get the job done by quick fixes. Our editors do not see the need for authors to be educated and aware and therefore anybody and everybody writes whatever they want and the readers read indiscriminately.

Whether something is fully expressed or not is not entirely dependent on the power of the author; it is also linked to the experience of the reader.

When people do not understand logical text, they are embarrassed. But most people blame the writer when they cannot grasp literature that is based on ideas. Not understanding poetry leads to a dismissal of the poet; it does not damage people's confidence in themselves.

True connoisseurs of literature are harder to find than writers.

When new literary creations emerge, the traditionalists are greatly offended; but if they like it they don't know how to react. They can't decide whether they should enjoy it or not.

When we analyse literature, there are two things to judge: how much of the world has the writer been able to internalize and how much of that has he been able to convey in permanent form.

The literary connoisseur can be recognized by his subtle understanding and empathy.

Judging literature is about explaining it and not about analysing it.

We can have a historical or theoretical analysis of literature; there may be a ritual need for such an analysis but there is no literary need.

One who sees literature correctly does not measure it but looks into its depth.

The lively literature of Europe has inspired our literary endeavours. The stronger it becomes, the more it helps us carve our own niche without imitation.

I can't understand the joy of reading a sickly book like *Anna Karenina*. I would like simple, beautiful, pleasant and generous writing. I can't tolerate petty, manipulative complications for long.

There are two or three epics in the world that have not dulled in a thousand years. Like water, they satisfy by quenching our thirst. They do not, like alcohol, take us to the height of excitement and then leave us dangling in dry despair.

Good travel literature is light and is the best to read at leisure.

The biggest advantage of travel literature is that it contains motion without the constraints of a plot; here, the mind has limitless freedom.

Nowadays, literary flavours in books written for children are greatly diluted with water; these books treat their readers as childish and not as young human beings.

Adhering to the fixed formats of periodicals is the work of the sad horse that pulls the tram car.

Keeping literature confined to the sensibilities of the tea-drinking crowd in genteel drawing rooms is like dressing nature in printed robes.

One cannot be a writer simply by defying rules.

If the poor pen had a consciousness, one day, while writing, it would surely think, 'I do all the writing but I get only ink on my face, while the reputation of the author brightens.'

Sometimes it is easier to orchestrate a war than a story.

When we speak through our pen, our words lose much of the energy.

The criticism of literature is called literary criticism, while most literature is really a criticism of life and nature.

If I write something and no one criticizes it, it is a heart-rending slight for a good book.

Books should belong to the person who reads books.

Modern literature contains some bottled truths, which in the hands of unskilled authors are becoming the 'curry powder' of reality. One of them is the melodramatic portrayal of poverty and the other is uncontrolled lust.

Europe seems to be obsessed with biographies. If they get a distant whiff of greatness, they will collect all the letters, conversations, daily events and other such garbage and try to publish a biography in two thick volumes.

There is no learning in the way we review literature. It is futile to say that this is good or that is not good. This gives us an opinion but not the truth behind a particular opinion.

There are many valuable gifts in the world but a letter is not the least of them.

Just as the peaks of the Himalayas contain so many floods within their rock-hard ice, who has locked the deluge of the human heart in this library?

LOVE

Where can you find a creature who is not worthy of love? Even wicked, grotesque people and sinners are loved by their mothers.

Even physical beauty glows through love.

When love happens it encompasses everything; if it does not, it is not love.

The eye of the lover does not blink.

The greatest gain of love is that it makes at least one person ideal in the lover's eye.

The meaning of love is not to surrender oneself. It means to give all that is good in oneself.

Love wants to see itself fulfilled; it is not so concerned with proving itself.

The biggest need a human being has is the need for love.

When we earn knowledge we are proud of it. When we are loved, we are humbled.

Only love can overcome fear, laugh in the face of danger, ignore loss and disregard death.

Human beings are so eager to love that eventually they will love their own idea of love.

It is not that love always distorts our perspective. Sometimes it helps to complete the perspective.

In the Bengali language two words are connected to love: 'love' and 'like'. They bear the addresses of the opposite shores of the sea of love. Someone else likes me, I love someone. When the emotion is facing towards me, it is liking and when it is facing towards someone else, it is love. Liking is about enjoying and loving is sacrifice.

Friendship means three things: two friends and a world. Together, two people can engage in worldly activities. Love means two people without the world. They are the world to each other.

Our hearts are close to some people in the world and only amongst them can we relax.

Memory is not about remembering the name; it is about keeping one in your heart.

MIND

Human beings are as extensive as the reach of their minds. If we are to be strong, our minds must be expanded.

The mind is a great entity; there is not much that the mind cannot do. It can disregard the chill of the south wind and walk quickly towards Burrabazaar. I accept that it can, but does it have to just because it can?

Our mind is the sum total of a few appetites: appetite for knowledge, joy and beauty.

My mind is not a mirror; it is the main instrument for creation. The moment I look at something, my mind helps to create. There are as many creations as there are minds. Seeing the same thing again, in a different mood, can lead to a different creation.

The human mind is like a bird with two nests: one is near and the other is far.

Is the human mind like a machine that it will work to a fixed schedule? The human mind is so various and detailed, moves along so many paths and has so many claims that it tends to move this way and that. This movement is the sign of its life, of humanity, and it is a protest against inertia.

The supreme power of the mind is not in its ability to remember everything; the ability to forget things that should be forgotten is also a sign of its strength.

There is one group of people who are overzealous because they want to understand everything in the world; another group is too eager to express all their emotions. Meanwhile, many things in the world continue to remain a mystery, and emotions stay pent up within the mind.

Whether it is in science or in art, the objective mind is the best vehicle.

When the mind has many objects to depend upon, it becomes lazy and overdependent on external factors. It forgets that in the celebration of joy, external factors are less important than inner ceremony.

The saddest moment of our lives is when the mind is bereft of desire.

When the mind becomes numb, we need to stir it in order to make it respond.

It is large houses that confine human beings more. The mind can ensconce itself there and the external world moves further away.

The call of the peacock is not sweet. However, under certain circumstances the mind can construe it as sweet—the mind has that power.

How have ordinary people kept their minds alive? It is mostly through rituals and habits. The immobile limbs of the mind are stuck together with the glue of habit; they are not unified by vitality of the spirit.

The primary joy of a scientific mind is of curiosity.

When stupor surrounds us, that is when we are in danger of losing something. When our mind is dormant, the external dangers are heightened.

Fear of ghosts is actually a fear of our own weaknesses. This 'fear of ghosts' constitutes the majority of our fears.

A person who does not change his mind when there is a conflict is like a mechanical doll. If we wind it up again and again, it will dance the same dance.

Only human beings claim: I am infinite. No other creature in this world makes such claims.

Man may be only five feet tall on the outside but his interior world can be so extensive.

If you ride on someone else's back and move forward, it is futile. The point is to learn to move independently, not to move ahead somehow or the other.

Old memories are like wine; the more you store them in your mind, their colour, taste and stupor become sweeter.

God had mercy on us and gave us the power to forget.

MORALITY

The lesson that you will die but you must not kill is most important; it is an imperative. It is not shrewd counsel or advice given for material gain.

Touching the feet of Brahmins and taking a dip in the Ganga are good things to do. On the other hand, honesty and truthfulness are also good deeds. Since there is no discrimination between one kind of good deed and another, the person who bathes in the river and does other daily rituals seems to be accorded more, not less, respect in society than the person who is honest and unmoved by temptation.

The weight of sin can break that which is brittle but the pain of repentance can create that which is permanent.

Modesty is a good trait only when it is sincere.

We need to remember that when complacence or ambition increase, destruction is inevitable.

Although many gentlemen will hesitate to steal, they will often borrow and never return what they borrowed. This, to them, is not stealing.

Animals can experience joy and pain but they cannot distinguish between good and evil.

If you are the only person in the whole world, your deeds are neither evil nor good.

MUSIC

Music begins where sentences end. Music is most influential where things cannot be articulated. What the sentence cannot utter, music can communicate.

When the music is great, there should be a pause in words. The success of the singer is revealed between words, while the author shows his expertise in words.

Even listening is a talent.

The audience, in our country, is happy to listen to the song. In Europe, the audience listens to the singing as well.

Our music is usually rendered by one person and it is for one person; but this does not mean that it is being performed in one corner. It is for the whole world.

Relationships between human beings are always marked by sadness, fear and prayer. The raga Bhairavi unlocks our hearts and releases those emotions. It connects our pain to the pain all around us.

Our Multan ragini is an afternoon melody. It seems to say, 'The day is done but nothing has been accomplished.'

Great ragas like Kannada and Todi have depth and sentiment that do not belong to a particular individual. The emotion they evoke belongs to that horizon where the lonely earth meets infinity.

I think that European music belongs to the daytime. It is a medley of quick harmonies including melodious and discordant notes, pieces and wholes. The night belongs to Indian classical music, a pure, sombre and unalloyed raga. Although they have opposite characteristics, both move us.

Music is about expressing emotions and not craft. Inasmuch as it expresses emotions, it is music. When it is too dependent on the craft, it is not music but something else.

Sanskrit is a dead language. Similarly, our classical music is also lifeless. They have lost their souls and only their bodies remain.

When music was in its earliest stages of evolution, it may not have had ragas but it did have noisy beats. The roar of such regular beats, more than tuneful music, can excite the uneducated mind.

While performing higher forms of music, there can be more mistakes. The iktara is simpler and so there is less scope for error. That does not mean that the iktara is superior.

Higher forms of classical music have their own sounds; they do not depend on Kalidasa and Milton for words. They can pick on mere 'tum ta na na' sounds and accomplish their goal.

In our country, wives acknowledge the superiority of their husbands and then dominate them. Music, here, too seems to follow words but then outreaches them.

It is sad that music is not part of our education. Music has no place in the factory cell called college.

The person who writes the song and the one who sings it can be sympathetic to one another but their creative powers will not be similar. If God had, during creation, simply built the skeletal framework and taken leave, asking someone else to add on the flesh and the fat, there would have been anarchy. In our country, the singer often tries to take the place of the songwriter.

Nowadays, people want to hear some particular music but not the ragas. For these songs, the gramophone is important. Now singers are popular amongst the younger generation because they know a few songs and not because they have mastery over music.

If we listen to the music that plays on the gramophone in every household and the music in the theatres, we can see the poverty of our souls being expressed. Not only that, we mistake that depravity for something precious.

The kirtan has the ability to express deep, dramatic feelings in a way that no other form of music can.

Vaishnav music is the music of freedom. It does not heed caste or creed. Yet, its restlessness is regulated by the soul and by beauty. It is not the wayward expression of the blind senses.

Many have melodious voices but few have the talent for singing. This is why many people can sing classical music but few can sing well.

Nowadays, when I listen to my songs, I cannot tell whether they are mine or not. The words may be mine but not the music. It is unbearable when the songs I have composed are not sung well. When one marries one's daughter to an undeserving man, one has to put up with disappointments; it is a similar experience for me.

I beseech you, let your singing be close to my songs; I should hear them and recognize them as my songs.

If you want to learn my songs, sing loudly, without hesitation, and sing to yourself.

NATIONALISM

It is better to serve the country through small, ordinary acts rather than by expressing grandiose intent.

The inhabitants of India can be roughly divided into Hindus and Muslims. We will make a big mistake if we think that we can ignore Muslims and sideline them in our efforts to build a nation.

When Hindus called the Muslims to join them, they did so in order to get the job done and not because they were dear to them.

We, Hindus and Muslims, have lived side by side for many hundreds of years, sharing the yield of the same field, river and sky. We speak in the same language; our joys and sorrows are one. Yet, we have not developed the humane relations that neighbours should.

The fact that Muslims can be turned against Hindus should be reflected upon. It is not important who has done so. Saturn, with its malevolent influence, can enter only when there is a crack. We need to be more careful of the crack than of Saturn.

We must admit that there is a conflict between Hindus and Muslims; we are not only separate; we are on opposite sides.

The perversion that is at the root of the Harijan problem as well as the problem with the Hindus and Muslims cannot be found elsewhere in the world.

Politics is not so dangerous in the hands of the Hindus. Delving into their history down the ages, it can be found that there is not much evidence of political unity. However, Muslims know what unity is and they are not strangers to politics either.

Right now if we build an Indian nation, it cannot be done by leaving out the Muslims.

When we stand in front of the Taj Mahal, we do not wonder whether it was built by Hindus or Muslims. We feel it, in our hearts, as the achievement of human beings.

When we are overpowered by differences within us, we cannot establish control. In such circumstances, others will dominate us; this cannot be stopped.

The first sign of loving one's country is knowing it.

However much we love our country, we never know enough about it.

Just because we are born in a country does not make it ours. Until we know our country, it is not ours.

Many people have said that the charkha will lead to swaraj; many have even believed it; but I have not met anyone who has clearly understood how.

The strength and glory of the country lies in its people's sentiments; it does not lie in money, administration or the skills of doctors and lawyers.

If in a country a poor man can aspire to be rich, that is a great hope for a country. That in our country many people are poor is not the entire story. The fact is that our country lacks hope.

How can we teach our countrymen to be rulers before we have taught them to be human?

It is unfortunate that it is easy to create rifts between countries but it is difficult to unite them.

Where we go wrong, our enemies will try to force their advantage. If not today, they will take advantage tomorrow; if one enemy does not, another enemy will. Therefore, we should try to correct our mistakes instead of blaming the enemy.

When our English-educated city-dwellers tell the illiterate villagers, 'We are brothers,' the latter do not understand the meaning of this brotherhood.

There is a huge chasm between us, the educated few and the majority of the population of our country. The squirrels had done a bit of work to build a bridge in the Treta Yuga; have we done even that much to bridge the gap between ourselves?

Just as no one can completely take away our country from us, similarly, no one has the power to give our country back to us.

Parliamentary democracy! If we bring it from a foreign pharmacy, will it match our needs and cure the ailments specific to us?

When the foreign rulers leave, our country will not automatically become ours. We will have to work hard to build our nation.

No nation can succinctly express what the national sentiment is, or what makes a nation work. This is something as obvious as the fact that the body has a soul; yet, like the soul, it is hard to define.

The good boys pass their exams, get good jobs and earn a big dowry in marriage. However, the country has high hopes from its naughty, disobedient and restless boys.

We know the people from Bihar, Marwar and Madras as others and not as one of our own. This is because the rituals that divide us are not based on our intelligence; in fact, they go against intelligence.

Our leaders have to prove that they can shoulder the responsibility of the country. We know their opinions but we have not seen their work.

A famous English poet has said that we eat the meat of foolish animals: goats, sheep and cows, for example. The Muslim conquerors had devoured us, the English are devouring us—there is no need for further examples.

Persuading the English to leave India by supplication or by force will not resolve our problems.

Our national consciousness lies in the fact that we do not worship nationalism as the ultimate truth.

We may not be soldiers, merchants or wayfarers but we can become well educated, mature, compassionate and humanitarian householders. Even if we are not rich, we can use our knowledge and love to help ordinary people too.

We are weakened by cliques, jealousies and pettiness. We cannot unite, we do not trust one another, and we are unable to accept the leadership of any amongst us.

On the one hand, we complain that the English do not give us the respect due to an equal; on the other hand, we beg for alms at their door.

Our current plight is such that we trust in nothing other than clerkship. We even treat business as madness. Applications are our safety nets and signing our names is indicative of valour.

A nation comprises a group of people who are bound together by common political interests.

Whether through lies or error, proving oneself as the best and other nations as inferior is the main characteristic of nations; it is the mainstay of patriotism.

We should not think that individualistic nationalism is the main objective of humanity. We must stick to the right path; humanity is certainly more important than nationalism.

Many of us think nowadays that all wrongdoing can be corrected through the touchstone of nationalism.

Today, the time has come when one must say that people belong to all countries and all times. There can be no distinction of nation or race amongst them.

The word 'national' has no definition; indeed, it is difficult to define. Different people decide what is national and what is not national depending on teachings and beliefs.

The existence of nations cannot be doubted but nationalism has many definitions. However, in the name of nationalism and worshipping of boundaries many lives have been sacrificed.

We have borrowed national pride from the west and it is tainted by excessive belief in national, commercial products. As a result, Indians today do not hesitate to say that national glory is more important than the glory of truth.

When city-dwellers think of the whole nation, their thoughts are confined to cities. Villagers do not know how to think of the nation at all.

All the stalwarts of the League of Nations do not want to stop the elaborate machinations of bullying; yet, they keep talking about peace.

NATURE

At dawn, I lose myself; at dusk, all other things seem to get lost.

To see the beauty of Bengal, one must ride on a boat amidst the placid waters of the Ganga during sunset, and enjoy the splendour of the western banks of the great river.

Nowhere in the world is the monsoon as beautiful as it is here in Santiniketan. And the ugliness of the monsoon in Kolkata, especially in Jorasanko, is also unrivalled in the world.

Here, in Sajadpur, the air and the landscape around me is filled with such languor, apathy, detachment but also a sweetness that I can't tell whether my mind is focused on something or whether it is completely scattered.

Monsoon is the season for holidaying. In India, monsoon was holiday time because there was an understanding between man and nature.

One can liken the monsoon to a Kshatriya king. His attendant announces his arrival with the deep echoes of the drum beat; he follows wearing a turban of clouds.

Summer is like a Brahmin. He suppresses all excess, purifies all, lights the fire of meditation and prays for salvation.

The blue-clothed night sky comes quietly and touches the earth softly; almost at once, our outer differences are blurred. We get an opportunity to experience the deepest bonds within us; that is why night is for love and togetherness.

Trees cannot become modern like human beings and therefore they are eternally fresh.

We live on earth and see freedom in the infinite skies; if your Himalaya range wants to encroach into that sky, like a bull with its horns, I cannot endure that.

Let me tell you why I don't like the mountains; when I go there it seems a bunch of mountain-keepers have locked up the sky and it has been tightly strapped up.

One important advantage of being friends with nature is that it gives happiness but does not demand anything in return. It does not want to secure that happiness until it is as tight as a noose. It frees human beings instead of trying to own them.

I have always felt that the day belongs to the earth but the night belongs to the heavens.

The day is marred by light; it is darkness that is unblemished. The dark sky is like the sea; it is as black but perfectly spotless. The day is like a river; it is not black but muddied.

The river moves constantly; that is why it is like our mind and consciousness.

The Ganga was one window through which one could see that the world is not confined to this city. However, the natural splendour of the Ganga is no more. It has been built up on both banks and straitjacketed such that the river itself looks like the sentry. If, once, it had any function other than transporting jute sacks on barges, it is not apparent now.

Indeed, in foreign lands, I feel closest to nature.

When we sit quietly in natural surroundings, we can feel in our hearts that being, not doing, is the ultimate ideal.

There is no shortage of space in nature; it is in our minds. See, the seed can contain an entire forest and an organism can carry its own lineage.

We see contradictions in every aspect of nature. But are they truly contradictions or are they two parallel truths?

There is no end to nature's work. But keeping that work in the background, nature expresses itself in being.

When nature tries to work towards its own objectives, it dwarfs the objectives of society.

The river gives water and fruit to the land. But most importantly, it gives movement. The river connects the land with those places that are outside or far and brings the vibrancy of motion into that which is inert.

There must be kindness somewhere in the intricate workings of nature; otherwise, where would we have got it from? However, it is difficult to locate exactly where the kindness can be found.

The life that we hold most dear to us has very little value for nature.

I love this gigantic earth that lies around us silently; I love it so much that I feel like grasping its trees, rivers, fields, sounds, silence, dawn and dusk with both hands.

I still love the earth in some ways but not in a detached manner. A ray reflects from the galaxy of my love and lights up all of humankind. That halo makes the earth look very beautiful and intimate.

I love this earth dearly. Its face has a far-reaching gloom; as if it remembers that it is the daughter of God but it does not have the power of God. It loves but cannot protect, begins but cannot complete. It gives birth but cannot rescue us from the clutches of death.

This earth and I have a relationship that seems to span ages and lifetimes and is therefore ever new. Both of us have a deep and extensive association.

Water has encircled the rugged earth as if in an embrace. The earth does not understand the innermost mysteries of the ocean. Water does not grow crops but in its absence, the earth would not have even one blade of grass.

The flowing currents of a river enable the transport of people and goods between one country and another. When the water dries up, the bed of the same river becomes a dangerous place. The river path of one time can become the path to destruction at another time.

It is the fittest who survive but there are many different kinds of fitness. Some survive because they are tough and others because they are tender. Some survive by holding their heads up, others by bowing. The tree survives in one way and the creeper in another.

The child wants to throw off its covers and we want to wrap it up with clothes. In fact, this war is not with the child but with nature. The natural knowledge deeply embedded within a child cries out in protest.

In nature, we see truth reflected in rules and joy personified in beauty. That is why truth is important to us but joy may or may not be.

Night falls after day and the day breaks after darkness; we should not deprive ourselves of the wonder of these phenomena just because we are used to them.

PERCEPTION

If we do not see things from a distance, the things that are great cannot be perceived as such.

When we see something from up close, we can only see one part of it. If we do not stand afar, we cannot see the thing in its entirety.

If we think we have it all, we have, in reality, lost it all.

We must acknowledge the existence of the finite as well as the infinite. When we see them as separate, we are trapped by illusion and then we make a mistake. We think we can get the infinite by crossing our finite boundaries: as if killing ourselves can bring immortality.

If we do not come out of something, we cannot fully get it. The child who is inside the womb does not get its mother; when it is born by severing the umbilical cord, it becomes a separate entity and gets its mother fully.

Influenza is like Abhimanyu; it knows how to enter but not how to depart.

It is more profitable to escape the stranglehold of one's attorney than to win the case.

A branch cut off from a tree has to be borne by people; a branch on a tree can bear the weight of people.

Youth is the horse and maturity is the rider.

When we see something in a disinterested way, or in the context of a need, we do not get a complete perspective. When we see something for the sake of seeing, we can see it completely.

A tree can bear good fruit. However, if the same tree also contains worms, we cannot judge the tree by the worms alone.

POETRY

There are no words in the dictionary for that which leads to a poem; the poet, therefore, skilfully uses everyday language to express himself.

In his youth, the poet tends to imitate indiscriminately. Eventually, when his talent develops, he finds his own rhythm. As he matures, he finds his own rhythm and then he can become immortal.

Do you know the difference between poets and other human beings? The gift of childhood, given by God, does not disappear for the poet. The mind and the eyes of poets are forever young, which strengthens their relationship with the evergreen earth.

The poet has exceeded the advice of the Gita. He has no right over his duties or over the results. His only control is over respite: respite from work and respite from consequences.

However great a poet is, he is never only a poet.

The day there will be no new poets in this world, we will know for sure that the old poets are completely dead.

Poetry is like a woman who does not bring good fortune. She gives happiness but no respite. When she welcomes someone she gives them intense pleasure, but at times her embrace is so tight that her heart can stop beating.

When someone listens to a poem and says, 'I did not understand anything,' he has to be told that there is nothing to understand; it is only a whiff. I have heard the reply, 'I understand that, but why a smell? What does that mean?'

A poem, first and foremost, has to be a poem. Even if it is not practical it is fine.

To write even a simple poem, one has to wring out one's emotions. Perhaps the reader does not understand any of that; he simply judges whether the writing is good or bad.

The world that poetry creates for us is very far removed from the reality of day-to-day life. This distance allows us to see the world of imagination and of eternal beauty.

Poetry wants to exceed its topic. It is the excess which is difficult to articulate.

When we read a poem, we enact it mentally. If those expressions do not enrich a poem, then that poem will not make its maker famous.

Teaching language through poetry is like shaving with a sword. We insult the sword and hurt the neck.

Composing poetry without rhyming words is not wrong but it is very difficult. It requires a special power.

Because of the rhyme, the words linger on. When the expressions cease, the experience does not. The rhyming words play with connections between the mind and the ear.

If flowing water is not bound by its shores on both sides, it does not look as picturesque. An unbound, uncontrolled pond is monotonous and bereft of beauty. For language, rhyme works as a shore by giving it a distinct form and splendour. The poem becomes a beautiful expression.

When we want to place a creeper on a straight wall, we need to nail it in some places to give support. Similarly, alliterations offer support to the reader's mind. Many lifeless compositions can be made captivating by this artificial means.

To be poetic is to have the ability to enter into your own, someone else's and nature's inner soul.

In some circles ineffective expressions such as silent poetry and inward emotion are bandied about. The wood that has not burned cannot be called fire; similarly, the man who stares at the sky and stays silent as the sky cannot be called a poet.

If I was born in Africa instead of India I would have been a different person. Similarly, if I was born with different poetical ancestors, rather than Valmiki and Vyasa, then too I would have been a different person.

When words and emotions are expressed through rhythm, it is poetry. When we take away the rhythm it is news.

All great poems have the power to invoke the sublime and guide us towards infinity.

All great poetry has something that satisfies our thirst for knowledge and also opens up our mind.

A poet or a lyricist has given us his poems and his lyrics, not his life. What shall we do with his biography?

In order to enjoy and understand a poem or a beautiful literary creation, we need peace and quiet. It is not something that can be done in a hurry. There is no way we can have a quick taste while moving from one task to another.

One must say this simple thing—what is sublime poetry can be poetry in verse or in prose.

It is better to write prose poems than to argue about them. Those who are objecting today will be imitating tomorrow.

When words do not come from pain but from other words, the craft of poetry becomes more complex and refined. The emotion that is not direct or deeply connected to the heart loses its simplicity.

Prose has practical uses but poetry, clearly, belongs to leisure.

Poetry is like a sea. Its variety is in the waves. But prose is like land; it contains the varied nature of forests, mountains, deserts and of plain and rugged landscape.

To be a poet, one does not need a lot of education.

REASON

When rumours start spreading, they need not be true. If five people say something, the sixth person does not refrain from repeating it. Logic is then replaced by recitation in many voices.

If logic does not take heed of proof, it is bad logic.

We need to survive by sometimes struggling with and sometimes compromising with reality. We cannot accomplish the smallest task by blindness or by cunning.

We must try and master that which is familiar; this gives us the strength to accept that which is unfamiliar and intangible.

However beautiful a simile is, it cannot be accepted as reason.

RELIGION

Religion will never let us forget what it means to be human. This is the main role of religion.

What can unite diverse groups of people? Religion.

The path of religion is precise but its ethics are simple and broad-minded. This path is permanent and belongs to all people; it is not the property of scholars and logicians.

The religion that we get from the Shastras does not become our very own; instead, we develop a habitual connection with it. It is the aspiration of our lives to give birth to religious feelings within us.

We need to remember that for spreading a religion, the religion is more important than the spreading. It's not that spreading itself can rescue the religion; if we protect the religion, it will spread by itself.

If we want to understand religion, we should see it in everyday life. Theoretical discussions can help to add to the historical elements but they do not help us grasp religion.

The clay with which the idol of the goddess is made is not real. Even if we adorn it with jewellery, it is not real. However, it would be wrong to say that the idol has no truth within it.

Religion and religious order are not the same thing.

Religion can be the path to freedom while religious orders encourage slavery.

Shastras are the records of traditional practices in the past.

Instead of being an internal thing, if religion prioritizes scriptures and external rituals then that religion can become a source of great discontent.

The distortions of religion can be dangerous; religiousness can cause more harm than squabbles over property.

Is religion to be found only in the pages of scriptures? Does God dwell only in the temple? Can God be found within those who deceive people?

Be good, love others and do good deeds for others, this is the way. Otherwise, where the rigidity of religious rituals, theories and traditions prevails, there the proponents of religion can indulge in petty quarrels that lead to murder.

Religion frees human beings and therefore religion needs to be non-partisan. But where religion gets caught up in factional rivalry, its petty sides get more prominence than its positive aspects.

The king who wants to enslave his subjects uses religion as a tool because religion robs human beings of clear vision. This religion is like a *femme fatale*—she enchants by her embrace and kills by enchantment. The power of religion can be more destructive to the human mind than that of weapons, since religion seems innocuous and comforting.

Great and illustrious men have founded religious sects. We, however, adhere more to the sect than to religion.

The repetition of meaningless ceremony has taken the place of religion amongst the people of this country.

Since our guru is like God, we touch his feet and consider ourselves blessed even if we know he is greedy for money.

Communal sentiments have caused more harm amongst people than material cravings. Money and property make people cruel and immoral but affinity to religion can cause far more injustice, blindness and brutality. History has proven this again and again, and nowhere can we get more ruinous evidence of this than in our everyday lives in India.

Communalism in religion is a contemporary phenomenon. Communal rulings compel people to hang on to ancient rites and rituals through the ages.

No communal religion has survived in its purest spirit. The structures that have held aloft these religions are rituals, beliefs and popular utterances from another time. Their ceremony and discipline impose one set of histories upon another, thereby obstructing the progress of religion.

At one time, as secretary of the Adi Brahmo Samaj, I had tried to establish global connections. When I saw that this was not possible since it was perceived to be a family matter, spending even one paisa on this seemed like a waste of money.

We know Christ though ordinary Christian missionaries. They have presented Christ to us through a veil of Christianity.

When the Sankhya philosophy was lively and active, our soul could gather life force from it. But now it is listless and has merely become a set of rules.

One can be a Brahmin simply by being born into a Brahmin family; our society has unquestioningly carried the burden of this lie, thus turning religion into a lifeless collection of blind beliefs.

Whenever human beings have tried to reduce the infinite according to their own convenience, using artificial rites and rituals, they have lost the treasure and tied themselves up in knots.

The nation that is named after a religion is bound to be chiefly recognized by its religion.

By worshipping our elders, we satisfy religion. This is because we gain blessings through all relationships and through those relationships we acknowledge the benevolent presence in the universe.

The reason for our unfortunate circumstances is in our religion.

People in our country believe in hating other human beings on religious grounds; they think their afterlife will be less glorious if they drink water from their neighbours' hands, and they insult others to maintain their superiority. Such people will always be humiliated by others.

We don't seem reluctant to accept the fact that things that are otherwise good and do not have any hint of evil in them can be considered wrong by the Shastras.

We don't believe in the religion we accept; we feel no sense of loss if we cannot accept the religion we believe in.

We are a respectful nation and being religious means to show respect. It seems pointless to us to judge who we are showing respect to.

Just as people make scarecrows in the fields to ward off the crows, religious rituals are often used as scarecrows to scare people.

RESPECT

We cannot be respected if we do whatever we please. A king cannot open a shop and run a business.

We cannot get respect through law.

One who does not know how to get respect will not be respected.

It was not our custom to build huge stone statues for great people after their death. We are not used to showing our respect through large slabs of stone.

When people are unequal, their getting together is not one of mutual respect.

When we imitate those who bare their fangs and show their claws, we give them respect. Ignore; do not imitate.

Respecting oneself gives power to the mind. It keeps the mind aloft and steers it towards work. The nation that loses self-respect loses the ability to move forward.

People who have a real thirst will go looking for water everywhere. When they get water, they will even drink water from their cupped palms. However, a person who is not really thirsty is only concerned about the value of the container. So, the water becomes unimportant, and there is squabbling over the container.

When you are jealous of somebody, you will use him but you will not feel any respect.

Disrespecting yourself is the basis of disrespecting others.

Placing an incompetent person in a high post is a way of insulting him.

Getting a right and having one is not the same thing.

We cannot do someone a favour just because we want to. We should also have the right to do it.

SELF

Work which is for selfish interest can be performed blindly but that which is for the welfare of people has to be done with conscious will.

If you cannot forget yourself, there can be no true union.

Even to be natural, one must practise.

It is not unknown to anyone that what we know ourselves as is often not accurate.

There is a space between who I am and who I am not. Identity is the naming of that space.

When you transgress your own nature, you become weak. The food of the tiger strengthens the tiger, but if the elephant was to be tempted by that, it would not be able to digest that food. We must not give in to temptation and wrong nature.

What we like moulds us, although we often do not know it.

Parents are thrilled with the new baby not because it looks beautiful but because it is truly theirs.

If I cannot control myself, other people will control me.

Just because we love our friends does not mean we have the strength to be friends. If we are to be friends, we must give of ourselves. Like all other charities, this too needs a fund; it is not enough just to wish to be friends.

The right to be by yourself is an important right. It has to be earned. It is difficult to get this right and to maintain it.

SIMPLICITY

If we lead a spartan life, we will see that a little comfort goes a long way and that comfort is not the only thing in life.

Something simple is not always simple for everybody; it is not simple for a goat to gather honey from a flower.

Simple things are good because their taste does not become old. Their simplicity keeps them young forever.

Complications signify weakness and failure; completeness is simple.

Simplicity is the only way to remain healthy. It is like the Ganga; if you bathe in it, the fever of the world can subside.

If we have to enter into the heart of a simple person, we must bow our heads to the height of his door.

A person with a good voice says, 'I don't sing well'; a good writer claims, 'I write rubbish!' The beautiful woman says, 'I am not good-looking.' These feelings should be discarded. They do not conceal one's pride nor do they express simplicity.

SOCIETY

The problem is not to erase differences and become one; it is to unite while maintaining our separate identities.

Society is larger than human beings.

There will be differences between one individual and another, one community and another. But the function of a social order is that such differences are not made rudely obvious.

If we must live together as one, then everyone's needs must be minimal. Moreover, every individual should have simple responsibilities that he believes in.

Where we are concerned only with ourselves, convenience and beauty have to be taken into consideration. Where society is also involved, these two things along with affordability must be kept in mind.

The war between Ram and Ravan was not about conquering lands but about protecting society. Sita was a symbol of that society. Ravan had abducted Sita, not the nation.

Human beings have complicated the social fabric of their lives so much that it has become very difficult to be happy and make others happy.

An injustice cannot be a permanent feature in any society.

Marriage is, like many other aspects of civilization, an attempt to unite natural desires and human objectives.

However great a person is, he will have many a debt to society.

A constant clash between two sides cannot be beneficial to society. Either one side perishes or both sides must unite.

Of the qualities that unite human beings, obedience is an important one.

Before we start applying for equality, we should try to bring about equality ourselves. Otherwise, we can be guilty of cowardice.

Selfish interest can bring us together but it cannot unite us.

Every day human beings are tiny, poor and alone—but on festival days, human beings become great by uniting with others and by realizing the strength of humanity as a whole.

True culture is about easy access, simplicity and plainness. Elaborate preparations indicate complexity and barbarism; they are the debris of failure.

We can exclude people in two ways: by ignoring them or by giving them excessive respect.

The fledgling bird does not have to graduate to learn to fly. It flies because it gets a chance to do so and it sees all others of its kind doing the same thing. Therefore it learns that it must fly.

Almost all dictates of human society assume that class is more important than truth.

If many people of modest means can pool their resources together, that can become seed capital.

A kind person opening a night school is like using tears to douse a fire.

If silkworms are dying or if grapes are being attacked by insects in Europe, they try to do something about it. In our country, we worship smallpox and cholera.

European music is never complete without a piano or an oversized organ. Similarly, European life is dependent on and never complete without heaps of commodities.

There is nothing more shameful and humiliating than the practice of dowry.

If we do not have joint families, we cannot have child marriage. If husband and wife have to live independently, they cannot be too young.

All human beings have two sides to them; on the one side they are alone and on the other they are connected to society. If we leave any of the sides out, we live under an illusion.

The book of Manu tells us how to behave with our mother, aunt and uncle or with Brahmins, Kshatriyas, Vaishyas, Sudras. However, it does not tell us how one ordinary human being should behave with another.

Diplomacy does not mean deviousness. What it really means is that one works according to opportunity rather than being driven by personal emotions.

SORROW

Sorrow does not necessarily cause harm to human beings; often, good things can come of sorrow, but sin causes grave injury to human beings.

We need to remember that sorrow is the opposite of happiness and not of joy. Sorrow is a part of joy. These words may seem paradoxical but they are true.

The game of chess is a game from start to finish. In the middle, there are moves and counter-moves and much tension. If that pain is not there, the game is meaningless. On the other hand, if the game does not provide joy, it is pointless.

The measure of sorrow is the measure of joy. We understand the sincerity of love by the amount of sorrow it carries. Of course there is sorrow, but sorrow exists because above all there is joy.

No one can create a heaven that has no blemishes or no sorrow.

Flowers have no sorrow; the misery of animals and birds is also limited. However, man's misery is of diverse kinds; it is deep and difficult to express. Within this world, it is difficult to understand the horizon of human pain.

Perhaps sorrow is an important ingredient of human life. To struggle, to strive, to sacrifice may be more important than to be happy.

In times of happiness, we assume that we have infinite power to be happy; however, in times of sorrow we see that the powers are not working.

We bear sorrows and troubles but we are not ready to bear responsibilities.

Sorrow belongs to human beings. God has taken on this sorrow as His own and united with human beings at the confluence of the sorrows. He has converted sorrow into freedom and joy—this is the essence of Christianity.

People can get annoyed when you show more sensitivity to pain than those around you. These others think you are trying to prove your superiority in some way.

There is no bigger deprivation amongst human beings than lack of sorrow.

Human beings have made much through sorrow. What is not constructed out of pain is not complete.

SPIRITUALITY

If the mundane issues of food and clothing are raised in a conversation regarding spiritual matters, they seem irrelevant. Yet, the spirit of the mind and the hunger of the body have always coexisted.

The essential theory of asceticism is not in its saffron robes but in the practice of its penance.

All great thoughts contain within them generosity and a spiritual consciousness.

What is deepest, highest and the most intimate within us is that which we cannot control. We cannot sell it or give it away.

That which is pure and free, that which is the best part of the soul, belongs to all human beings; it is not the property of illegitimate owners within the closed doors of a temple.

There are three kinds of values: one is that of practical needs and it belongs to the marketplace; another is that of religious needs and is connected to society; the third is that of the spirit and it is personal.

If there is no spirituality in a race, human beings cannot achieve greatness. Those who know the history of their love, their service and their sacrifice cannot claim that there is no spirituality in the west.

A saint looks for a place uninhabited by human beings for his meditation. But he does not look for a place without animals and birds; why is that?

TIME

Satya Yuga was never a thing of the present; it has always been part of our past.

If a person does not love the time he is living in, he cannot do good work that is relevant to that time.

Earlier, there wasn't such a great divide between the educated and the uneducated. Then, one person knew more and the other knew less. But now, the enlightened person knows one thing and the ignorant knows another altogether.

It is misleading to apply the utterances of the Shastras to contemporary times as they are not relevant any longer.

Pure is the sweetness of the past. We sigh as we say we have lost our past but the past has also taken away much that is ugly and sad. That which is sorrowful is not the past, it is wasted. Only that which is happy and beautiful is the past.

There is nothing as transient as novelty.

The old and the antique are unending sources of novelty.

The difference between the new and the novel is that every era has some novelty. The new is, however, something that is beyond the transience of time.

Just because a person is familiar, we cannot always close our eyes and recall every detail of their face. Incidents which were very important at one time can at other times be difficult to bring to mind.

When people start growing old, they start criticizing the present in comparison with the past. This is because their past is linked with hopes and the present with settling accounts.

TRUTH

When a child is born, it is weak. When truth comes in the garb of a child, we can place our trust in it. If truth is born with a beard and moustache, then it has to be taken as a distortion.

Money and wealth create divisions; only truth has the power to rise above these.

If we accept truth blindly and unquestioningly, that truth has no value. Like Sita, truth will have to stand trial by fire again and again.

Even if truth is old it is still the truth and even if we misunderstand it, it still remains the truth.

A person who lies has to say many things but the person who is speaking the truth need not say more than a word.

Only when one is completely guided by truth can one fully realize its power.

What is true may not be easy.

All that is true—in other words, all that is real and permanent—cannot be rootless. It exists because it exists within an order.

Partial truth can often be a falsehood.

Using truth to boast is to insult truth.

If you do not have the freedom to make mistakes, you cannot discover truth.

When the dream shatters, truth loses nothing.

Science is not connected to individual natures. It involves objective curiosity about the truth.

Where customary practices mock the truth, such practices are shameful.

While truth gives us patience, opinion robs us of it.

Many philosophers have dismissed the real world as a dream. But the same philosophers have not been able to negate dreams. Therefore, it is obvious that with forceful logic it is possible to dismiss truth but not dreams.

Relationships based on need are about gain. They include greed, not joy. The relationship based on truth is about give and take because only joy can give generously.

To us, words are more important than the truth.

At the time of excitement, excitement seems like the greatest truth.

VIOLENCE

Force does not have the perfection of wholeness. It destroys the uniformity of the whole and shows itself up as separate. Therefore, it may seem to stand out but it is actually insignificant.

We are the most harsh where we ourselves are incomplete. It is in this regard that we are cruel to others and others' cruelty pinches us the most.

Where it is a question of needs, force can be used. Food snatched and eaten can satisfy hunger. But where the will is not linked to any needs, it is found in its purest essence and cannot be forced to do anything.

When people want to prove something that is not natural they start screaming louder. They forget that a discordant note in a mellow tune may escape our notice but in a loud song, it will stand out.

To show power is not an evidence of power.

If we forcibly push away the causes of unrest, we cannot bring peace. This causes unrest to thrive elsewhere.

A man who is drunk can kill but he cannot fight a war.

The difference between strength and excitement is that between a flame and its embers.

Just as some miscreants cannot work unless they have imbibed alcohol, similarly hatred cannot work intensely unless it is blind.

Force knows only itself. It does not accept the existence of any other.

WEALTH

No one in the world has so much wealth that they can rightly say, 'I am wealthy.'

Where there is no true hospitality, there can be no wealth.

The ultimate aim of wealth is not to remove poverty but to make one realize divine greatness.

If we cannot get the full worth out of something, then the money is wasted and we do not get the thing either.

We do not get anything valuable through the mercy of others; we must acquire it by our own strength. It simply cannot be otherwise.

The person who says 'I do not have the resources' is poor. But can the person who says 'I do not need this' be called poor?

A purely materialistic person is an uncivilized person.

To give to another is the biggest gift one can give oneself.

People who limit their achievements to the acquisition of power can attain wealth but not God.

The essence of prosperity or poverty lies not in material resources but in the character of human beings.

If we cannot give something away, we do not own it completely.

The heaviest vessel is an empty begging bowl.

At one time, human beings could ignore money for the sake of humanity; now they ignore humanity for the sake of money.

The nature of wealth is iniquitous.

There is a vast difference between Lakshmi and Kuber. Lakshmi symbolizes prosperity; she accumulates wealth by looking after the well-being of all. Kuber is all about acquiring; he increases wealth through accumulation.

Commerce is one of the ugliest things in the modern world. It has deadened the earth by its crushing weight and deafened it with its loud noise. It has polluted the environment with its filth and damaged the earth with its greed.

Contemporary civilization is based on exploitation. The minority want to feed on the majority and expand their wealth. This causes some individuals to prosper but does not help the larger majority to live a better life.

Basically, those who want to hide their debts have not been able to convert their loans into wealth. The debt has remained a debt.

No race can make progress only though material accumulation of wealth and it cannot acquire power through materialistic wisdom. If we add large quantities of oil to a lamp, it will not light; neither will it light if we only have the skill of making the wick. Somehow or the other, fire has to be lit.

Once we start to save, we become machines for saving. Our savings then surpass our needs and in fact start to trouble our needs.

Too many commodities are the main barrier to the full development of life.

The inspiration for modern-day politics is not pride but the lure of money. We need to remember that people can help to enhance the glory of the state but they cannot relate to heads of state acquiring individual wealth.

WOMEN

Women have great similarity to water. Both can flow and sparkle. They have an easy rhythmic movement which is lyrical. They can pour themselves into any container. They can dry up in sorrow or heat but strong blows do not destroy them completely.

The new bride gives up everything; her tears are witness to that.

Neither men nor women have more or less demands on the wealth of life. It is their undivided wealth.

The power that women have over men's hearts is called 'shakti' in our country.

Women are the bridge between the past and the present; men are the bridge between the present and the future.

Women are naturally skilful. Men are lazy by nature; they work out of compulsion. Women have a lively resourcefulness that naturally expresses itself in efficiency.

Patriarchal society has wasted and distorted the power of women. In trying to control women, men have created even more suffocating bonds for themselves.

All the high ideals of marriage seem to be more applicable to women than to men.

If we take the woman out of the entire human being, and grant her special rights, then we are depriving the whole of humanity.

Young girls have to learn to respect a person called a husband. Through many rites and rituals that involve worshipping, this respect permeates the entire being of the woman. When she finally gets a husband, she thinks of him as a husband and not a person.

There is natural love between men and women. In our country, there is an attempt to bypass this and create an ideal of domestic love between husbands and wives.

However tough the husband is, he wants not only obedience from his wife but he also wants her heart.

WORK

Discipline helps accomplish the task, but unity can bring spirit into it.

Sometimes, like lightning, the thought strikes me that all of this so-called important work—lecturing, writing, pretending to work for the country—all of this is unnecessary. All of this makes life divided, unconnected and incomplete.

Along with development comes the manifestation of differences within unity.

There is no burden heavier than an empty day.

Not everyone in the world can value leisure; to some, leisure is nothingness.

Money is not food; we need to buy food with money to be able to eat. Similarly, enthusiasm alone does not make us successful. We need to convert enthusiasm into work to achieve results.

There is nothing more beautiful and great than simply carrying on with the daily tasks of one's life.

I don't think there is any need to make hideous the hustle-bustle of work with such deliberateness.

Not only do wheels move with the help of force and fuel, they also have their own motion. Similarly, the wheels of work are set in motion by people but work has its own speed as well. Work forges ahead through more work.

The work done out of a sense of duty is fleeting. Work that is created out of play has the stamp of permanence.

The preface to work is knowledge. It is important to understand, first of all, the conditions of the workplace.

The person who is enthusiastic about work does not need flattery.

Just because I wish to work, and my work is not wrong, doesn't make the conditions of work easier.

People who are too focused on work can miss out on the glory of the wider world.

Just as the engine needs steam, people need motivation to work.

Nowadays, we often lie about the dignity of labour but in our heart of hearts we know that certain kinds of work are degrading.

Great work, like a large forest, requires a lot of space. This time is called inactivity, detachment or meditation.

Sometimes we waste more time doing trivial things than in doing nothing at all.

Prosperity is determined to favour the brave and therefore she has spread waves of fear amongst human beings. If you can cross them, she is yours. Those who sit on the shore and are lulled to sleep by the sound of the waves, or those who cannot steer their boat and cross the seas, are deprived of her riches.

Indian civilization has not differentiated between duty and work. Therefore, in our country, work is one's moral duty. We say that the ultimate aim of work is to achieve freedom from work and it is our moral duty to work towards this freedom.

Excitement is hungry for fanfare and fanfare is notorious for wasting time.

Human beings have two arenas of work: one is that of necessity, the other of pleasure. Necessity is external and is linked to a need. The urge for pleasure comes from within and is linked to feelings.

Undoubtedly, many people waste time by not doing any work but some others also waste time working; this spoils the work and wastes time.

Where would the glory be if there was no criticism? I embark on some great work and if it has no detractors, what is the value of that work?

The ethics of duty does not say that you should decrease your own load by giving the major share to others.

It is impossible to create barriers for the person who is committed to his work.

Where I have got something based not on my hard work but on the mercy of others, that charity does not benefit the giver or the receiver.

Trading enhances skills but sensitivity is abated. The person who makes sweetmeats cannot eat them.

It is characteristic of modern times to judge work by its extent and not by its depth.

The more varied, immense and powerful the task, the greater is the need for dedication and discipline.

Dutifulness may be a great thing but when it begins to overpower everything it belittles human beings. This is an inconsistency because the human soul is larger than the work of human beings.

The salary is not the main reason for doing a job; it is happiness we seek. We use money to attract that happiness in artificial ways.

When people shirk work, they cannot see it themselves.

Someone who does no work requires constant praise. The wealthy man who has no achievements and no work has the greatest need for flattery.

THE WORLD

Some complain that this world created by God is imperfect. However, if it were not, our subjugation would be complete. We would be dominated completely and we would have no control over the world.

If a person rejects his own home, the world will not come to his house as a guest.

All things in motion have one goal, which can be reached by different paths. All rivers are going towards the sea but not all waterways become one river; this variety, of course, is good for us.

The same force that brings the river into the desert will propel it towards the sea. He who makes us commit a blunder will rescue us from it. This is how we carry on.

When you lose your dynamism, your destruction will begin; you will be motionless but others will not stop. If you cannot keep pace with the world, the momentum of the world will crash upon you. You will be shattered or you will be worn down, little by little, and disappear.

What fate gives us is proportionately distributed; if we are given plenty in one area, there will be something lacking in another.

Twin forces can be beneficial when they balance each other; for example, gravitational force and anti-gravitational force, self-interest and the interest of others, self-improvement and the improvement of the surroundings. Otherwise the surroundings rise in revenge and barbarism destroys civilization.

In this ancient world, only beauty and things of the heart do not age. That is why the world is youthful and the poet's verse is never completely exhausted.

We do not hunt deer because we have something against them. We are forced to kill them because the poor creatures live deep in the forest and are swift runners.

There is no one as poor as he who must live on the streets.

However big a pitcher is, even if it has a tiny hole, it is useless. Then, that which had kept you afloat can drown you.

Everybody will unanimously accept that there is nothing as convenient as Aladdin's magic lamp. The only problem is that it is not available anywhere.

Let's go! Keep moving! Move like the cataracts, the waves, the morning bird and the early light of the sun. This movement is the reason for the vast and varied universe and for the infiniteness of the sky.

The university in Santiniketan will be a conduit between India and the whole world. Here, we must educate people to be global citizens; the days of narrow national confines are over. The initial preparations for the great international assembly of global citizens are being made in this corner of Bolpur.

The western continents have alienated the larger world with their politics and tempted it with their science.

Compared to my own countrymen, Americans have welcomed me as one of their own.

When we are impressed by the increased splendour of a country, we focus on its achievements and success but we overlook the difficult paths of its struggle.

When the Ganga is at its source, it has one fixed path. Then when a number of tributaries and distributaries come and join it, the river advances towards the sea and its form changes. That pristine, crystal-clear water becomes murky. Yet, no one says that the Ganga should re-trace its path back to its source because the waters are tainted and the river does not have its original force. This is because it is important to look at the entire picture that comprises everyone and everything.

ABOUT MYSELF

I wish to welcome every sunrise in my life and bid goodbye to every sunset as to a friend.

When I was younger, I could not wait to see my writing in print. Now, with age, even if my writing is not in print, it does not seem that the world has lost much.

In this life, poetry is my first love; I cannot bear to part from it for long.

If I could write a poem every day, my days would pass happily. But although I have been working at this for a while now, writing poetry is not something I am able to control; it is not that mythical horse, which can be harnessed every day.

Sometimes composing poetry makes me happy. At other times, writing a poem can leave a wound in the mind. That spot, then, feels sore again and again.

It is not that I can write all my good poems at will. If I lose even one of those lines, I doubt I will be able to compose it again even if I tried very hard.

Consciously or unconsciously, I may have done many things that were untrue, but I have never uttered anything false in my poetry: that is the sanctuary for the deepest truths of my life.

To this day, I have not understood how I wrote the *Gitanjali* in English and how people appreciated it so much.

Nature and music have an intimate relationship. I know that if, right now, I stand near the window and start singing a few notes of the Ramkali raga, then this sunny, blue-green horizon will, like an enchanted gazelle, come close to my heart and lap it up.

Let my paintings prove that I am not one hundred per cent Bengali but also European, to an extent.

The intimate relationship between me and the external world is not as clearly expressed anywhere as in my letters.

In Santiniketan, I had wanted to create an ideal life. Students and teachers together would create a complete entity—this was my objective.

I despise false imaginativeness. I can see the pragmatic aspect of everything. But even in the pettiness and conflict within things, I sense some unarticulated celestial mystery.

In the western hemisphere, my wheel of fortune follows the course of fame but in my own country it faces derailment at every step.

Even though my mastery over English is less than many other scholars in our country, I have been able to find a place in English literature. Many people will not be able to accept this simply and with generosity of spirit; neither will they be able to forgive me for this.

After my death, my countrymen should not create farcical commemorative tributes in my memory. I am grateful for what I have received in my lifetime.

In England, mischievous children tie bells to the tail of a dog for their cruel pleasure. By awarding me the Nobel Prize someone has tied something to my name. Whenever I move, it makes a clanging noise.

I have welcomed the whole world as my country.

The lived ideal of my life is that whenever a responsibility has come upon my shoulders, I have not neglected it but borne it with fortitude.

I have believed in courtesy, not as a social dictate but as something that naturally evolved from within. I do not call it nobility but humanity.

In his own creative field, Rabindranath is alone; no history has tied him to that which is popular.